Debt Free: Overcoming Debt And Regaining Financial Freedom

by

Maurice Chavez

Copyright © 2019 Innovate Media

All rights reserved. No portion of the book may be reproduced or utilized in any form or by any means, electronic or mechanical, including photocopying, recording, or by any other information storage and retrieval system, without express written permission from the author.

Table of Contents

Background 5

Introduction 9

Chapter 1 Knowing Yourself, Knowing Your Enemy 11
    Knowing Yourself 11
    Enticers to Debt-The Enemy Tactics 13

Chapter 2 Assess Your Current Financial Standing 17
    Know Where You Are 17
    Incorporating Your Family at the Start 18
        Pension 21
        Personal possessions/art/antiques 21
        Insurance 21
    Assets – Liabilities = Net Financial Worth 22

Chapter 3 Knowing Your Expenditures 23

Chapter 4 Envisioning Your Financial Future; What is Your Dream? 28

Chapter 5 Merging Your Dreams/Financial Goals with Your Expenditures 32
    Creatively Reduce Expenditures 34
    Build Your Savings 35

Chapter 6 Tackling Debt 36
    Top-down Method 37
    Bottom-up Method 39

Chapter 7 Have a Strategic Plan 41
    Parts of a Strategic Plan for Your Financial Goals 43
        Mission Statement 43
        Vision Statement 43
        Values and Principles 43

SWOT Analysis 44

Smart Long-term Objectives 45

Smart Short-Term Actions/Objectives/Initiatives 45

Score Card 46

Chapter 8 Ways to Watch Out for Wasting Money 47

Wasting Food 47

Bad Habits 47

Designer Clothing for Babies 48

Gambling 48

Unclaimed property 48

Unclaimed Tax Refunds 48

Interest on Credit Cards 49

Wasted Energy 49

Daily Coffee Intake 49

Speeding and Traffic Tickets 50

Chapter 9 Big Mistakes You Should Not Make 52

Thinking "Everyone is doing it"-Credit Cards 52

Do not assume that you can pay off your debt without making a plan for it. 53

Negotiating on Rates? What about Debt Settlement Companies? 54

Having a Wrong Attitude 56

Chapter 10 Finding Support for Your Journey to Financial Freedom 57

Summary 59

Appreciation 64

Background

Americans are drowning in debt. While this is sad, it is the true story in many homes in America. By the time the recession hit, many households were treading in dangerous waters, but economic times have grown increasingly difficult ever since. The rate of unemployment has continued to skyrocket, and the amounts that investors expect from their investments have continued to dwindle.

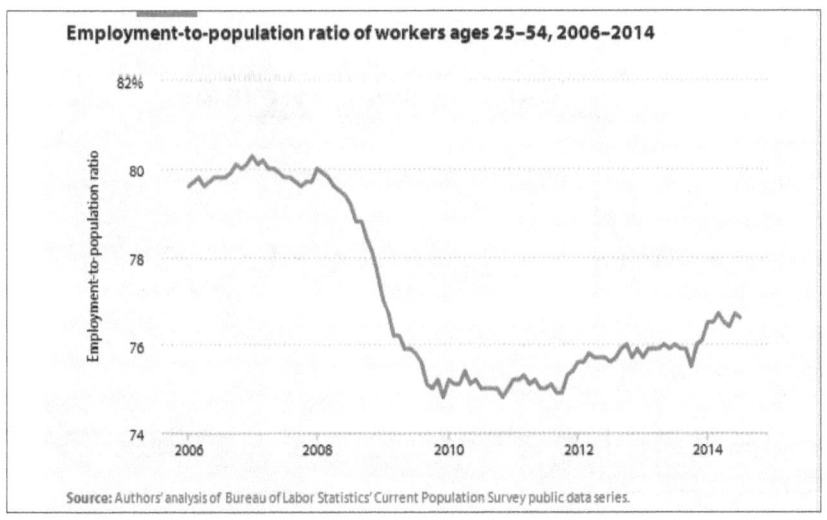

In such an environment, those with the greatest debts were not able to keep up with paying their debts, and many have sunk because of this. Still others have continued to be forced into solvency/foreclosure and bankruptcy.

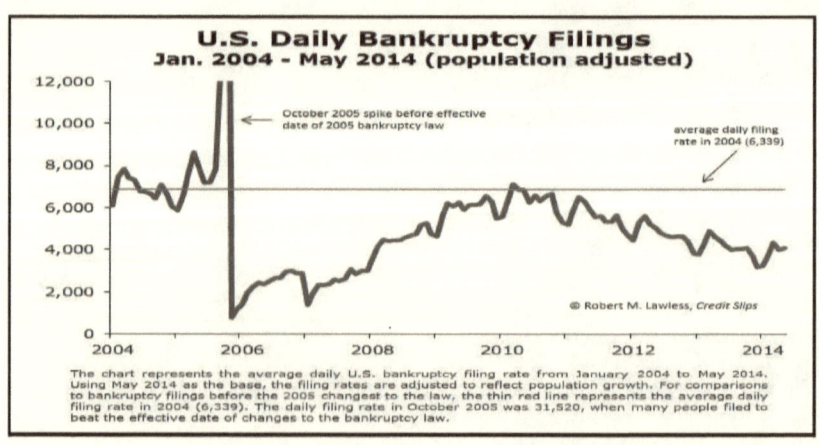

The figures in 2011 were up; bankruptcy filing stood at 1.4 million and foreclosure at 7.6 million (2009-2011). Mortgage delinquency in July of 2012 was 7.58%, and the ratio of homes that were foreclosed was 1 in every 69 homes.

As of August 2014, debt statistics revealed that, on average, American households have their credit standing at $15,480. Mortgage debt is $156,474, and student loans at $33,424. While this is the average for the whole US, particular states are affected by unique features that raise their average credit standing.

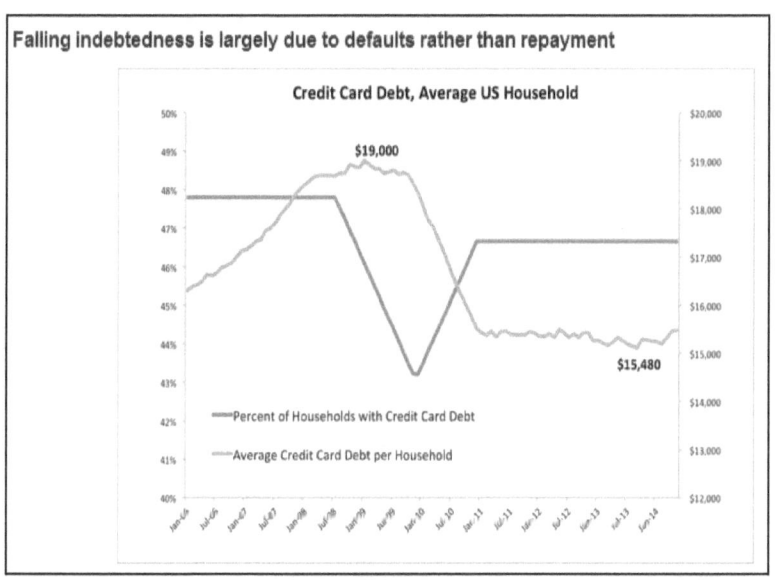

There is a possibility that you identify with these kinds of figures, either with the greater percentage or the lower percentage. As you have seen, you are not alone. Many Americans are in the same boat. And remember, debt is not through and through negative; through debt, many have been schooled, bought houses, and acquired property. But, on the other hand, unpaid debt can easily cripple you to the end of bankruptcy and bring with it much turmoil. It is not a wonder that more than 70 million Americans are on one drug or another! Stress levels, depression, and violence are on the rise among many Americans. Most of this could be resolved with the peace that comes from being debt-free. And while there are millions of Americans in debt, the effect heavily weighs on you as an individual; it is time that you break free from your financial prison and simply enjoy the freedom, peace, and satisfaction that come with being debt-free.

Introduction

You can be free from all your debt. There are many myths that people buy into that tell them why they may not be able to get out of debt. Some of these include: "Only rich people can be debt free," "The amount of my debt is just too high," and "I have too many other expenditures that I can't afford to settle my debts."

Consider the following letter we received from Miriam:

> "I want to get out of debt; I have $75,000 between credit card debts and student loans. I want to be serious about how I handle my money. I have been reading blogs, but I haven't yet gotten ahold of one particular way for me to get out of debt. In my youth, I never developed good spending habits; this has caught up with me in my adult life, and I am sinking deeper and deeper. Every attempt at getting out of debt seems to fail at the start. Kindly help me."

Many can identify with Miriam. Debts are real, and they seriously impact the health of those who owe money. Sitting and mulling over the fact that you have debt will only drug you into a negative spirit, drain you of your energy, and cripple whatever resources you could otherwise use.

You can do it! A journey of a thousand miles starts with one step, and the first cut paves the way to the many other cuts that will finally fell a huge tree. Once you have taken your first steps, then you are able to build momentum that will see you through the rest of the journey to freedom.

This book is here to suggest practical steps that many have taken who now are free of any debt. They are now investing and planning for their retirement.

Miriam has been utilizing the tips in this book, and this is how she explains her experience:

"It's now been almost a year, and, while my income has not changed a bit, I have managed to pay more than $10,000 in debt. Now that I have taken baby steps and have grown stronger, I look forward to the next year with great anticipation and hope of doubling this figure and even going beyond the doubling. It has worked for me, and I know I am becoming debt-free."

Chapter 1
Knowing Yourself, Knowing Your Enemy

Knowing Yourself

So, how did you get yourself into "this amount of debt?" My friend and I were freshmen at the time we got our first credit cards. And since there isn't much freedom with being freshmen, we at first didn't have much to spend our credit card money on. But, as time

went by and, one by one, we gained our freedom, there were more and more opportunities to explore the outside world. By the time we became seniors, we were pretty much free to go out as much as we wanted. Being freshmen restricted us to a particular stipend, and we weren't allowed to have outside jobs. This left us with our the credit cards. And, as we neared our graduation year, we rationalized that we were soon to start earning the "Big Money," and so we literally spent all that there possibly was on the credit cards. At the time, we silenced every thought that crossed our minds that seemed to say, "You are spending your future on a not-so worthy lifestyle."

Every time I wanted to spend my credit card on my extravagant lifestyle, I realized that there was something like a "battle" in my mind. There was one part that seemed to be "the responsible adult." This part was often thoughtful and rational. But there, too, was the other part. It would often find reasons as to why I should have fun. Too much study without play makes Jack a dull boy!! Have fun and have it now or never! I like to call this the "monkey mindset."

Every human being has two main parts to their mind. Scientists call these two parts of our brains the prefrontal cortex, which is the part of the mind that acts responsibly, and the limbic system (monkey mindset), which wants fun here and now!

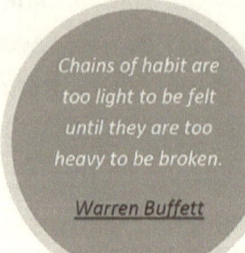

There are times when either the monkey mindset wins or the responsible mindset wins; it all comes down to the choices you make. Remember the moments when you have thought such things as, "Eating chocolate during the holidays does not count for much: I will soon be back on my diet"? Then, when you get home, you have yet another excuse for not sticking to your diet. The monkey mindset (limbic system) wins! When you decide you want to carefully consider your expenditures and gain control of your money, however, the responsible part of your brain wins.

Enticers to Debt-The Enemy Tactics

ಸಿ‌ಞ

*Know your enemy and
know yourself and you can
fight a hundred battles
without disaster.*

Sun Tzu

ಸಿ‌ಞ

Issuers of debt usually base their sales strategies on the monkey mindset to make sure you buy from them. Here are some of the "wise" ways used by debt issuers in conjunction with the monkey side of the brain:

- **Reframing an Issue**: I remember the day I wanted take out a loan to buy a car. When I walked into the dealership, everyone was smartly dressed and quick to help me see that I could own virtually any car in their showroom. One salesman was quick to ask, "What kind of payment do you want to make for this car? There is this mode of payment that is manageable, cheap, and tolerable!" I then started to agree with him that I could own any car. Two years down the line, the loan was not anywhere near clearing. I had other, better things to do with my money, but I still had a very large chunk of the loan to clear. The salesman's question should have been, "What is your budget?"

- **Discounting Hyperbolically:** This is when you choose to fulfill the here and now at the expense of the future. Remember when I was a freshman and chose to spend all there was on my credit card on the basis of the "Big Money" that was yet to come? But, when the "Big Money" finally came in five years down the line, my future already had the burden of thousands of debts.

- **Now or Never Mindset:** My friend and I went looking for a house for her. We found one in a very nice location that was exactly what she wanted. Unfortunately, it was out of her price range. Since it was just what she wanted, we kept thinking just how hard it is to find a perfect house, and we were tempted to find ways of getting her the house, anyhow. As I look back, I thank God that someone else was able to pay up and buy the house before we went into further debt over it!

The above is a brief analysis of just who we are and points at some of the things that might have contributed to our going down the path to debt. The bitter truth is that we participated in choosing to get ourselves into debt.

To better understand yourself, you will also need to ask some questions that relate to your being in debt:

- Who?
- What?
- Where?
- When?
- How?

Getting out of Debt; Overcoming the Monkey Mindset

1. The first step to getting out of debt is to know just how much debt you have. List, down to the last detail, everything you owe. Then, take a hard look at yourself and tell yourself: **I am in_____ amount of debt because I got myself into it!** It sure is a hard thing to do! But this makes for a very important step in your getting out of debt.

2. **Write up a contract with yourself; have your signature at the top and plan to pay.** This is a contract that accepts that you are in debt and that you commit to pay off the debt. Here is something that I did:

> 6th Nov, 2008
>
> **Contract on settling debt**
>
> I Miriam Gorge, here by acknowledge that I owe $75,000 in debt and commit to paying up the whole amount-in 7 years to come.
>
> So help me God.
>
> Miriam

3. **Reaffirm yourself.** You cannot afford to condemn yourself. All of us make mistakes; be quick to accept your mistakes. You can feel guilty and work towards changing whatever caused you to be guilty, but avoid beating yourself up. Seek to change what needs to change and get back to your plan.

4. **Reward yourself** when you make progress.

5. **Start somewhere!** The contract worked for me, and I also took the action of clearing my first debt.

6. **Find a support group or an accountability partner.** Thankfully, there are many sites and forums on which people who are fighting debt can meet. There are also those who have overcome debt and could be great examples to encourage you and help you believe in yourself. If others have done it, you can do it, too.

> "No one is free who has
> not obtained the
> empire of himself. No
> man is free who cannot
> command himself."
> — <u>Pythagoras</u>

CHOOSE FINANCIAL FREEDOM-GO FOR FINANCIAL FREEDOM

Chapter 2
Assess Your Current Financial Standing

Know Where You Are

Before you worry about how you will ever clear the huge amount of debt that is overwhelming you, you need to find out just how much debt you have. Otherwise, you may end up having anxiety and stress over something you do not have details/knowledge about. I realized that, once you get down to writing up your finances, you start feeling good. Then, the solutions come in, and the problem no longer seams as big.

The year prior to my deciding that I was starting my journey to freedom, I was always anxious and fretting. While statistics were high on foreclosures as well as bankruptcy, the fact that my acquaintance's mother was facing foreclosure jolted me into wanting to do something, whatever it took.

So I decided to do a thorough analysis of my financial situation. I chose to list all the debt I had, all the income I had, all the expenses that I was expected to meet, and any other detail that involved my finances. The document below is a financial net worth statement. This statement gives you a preview of just how you are faring with your finances. If your financial net worth has been declining over the years, then you have reasons to jump into action so that you can reverse the trend of eroding your wealth. But if your financial net worth statement has been positive and appreciating over the years, you are safe; keep going in the right direction.

Incorporating Your Family at the Start

Before you start to fill in this document, it is important that, if you are part of a couple or a family, you should take time to talk with your partner or family members. Most families find time to discuss their vacation trips and other things, but fail to discuss their family financial issues. Involve as many family members as possible. This way, you will be able to implement your recovery plan much more easily without resistance from your family. You will also get the much-needed support of your family members when times get tough, since they will be sharing in the family financial goals and changes.

Whereas there is still a debate as to how soon families should incorporate their children in financial planning, I take the position that children should be incorporated into family financial planning so that they are able to start learning fiscal responsibility at a much earlier stage. You know the saying that goes, "Train a child in the way that he should go, and when he is old, he will not forsake your ways"? This has worked for many. My friend's father took this initiative and sat her down to talk about money when she was only 12. Even though he had not had any proper education, he seemed to know just how to manage every coin in the family and still save for such activities as family vacations in Switzerland, while making sure they all had what they needed. They were not as rich as we were, but they often enjoyed much more than we did.

You could also choose to have all the necessary documents that relate to your finances readily available so that you can easily refer to them as you fill in the "My Net Financial Worth" plan.

My Net Financial Worth

My Name_____

Date_____

My Cash and Deposit Accounts	
	Amounts
Savings	
Checks	
Sales from private business	
Other sources	
1.	
2.	
TOTAL CASH AND DEPOSIT ACCOUNTS	

My Outstanding Debt

	Financial institution	Amount
Credit card 1		
Credit card 2		
Car loan		
Mortgage		
Any other loan		
Home buyer's financial plan		
Total		

My RRSPs and Non-RRSPs

My RRSPs

	Financial institution	Amount

Non-RRSPs

	Financial institution	Amount
GICs		
Stocks		
CSBs		
Mutual funds		
Employee share purchase plan		

My principal residence	
Mortgage company	
Current home value	
Mortgage balance	
Interest rate	
Mortgage payment	
Frequency of payment	
Maturity date	

Vehicles		
	Type	Worth
1		
2		

Pension_____

Personal possessions/art/antiques_____
_____
_____

Insurance_____

Once you have your detailed financial standing, you could choose to summarize your information in a concise template.

	ASSETS	LIABILITIES
INVESTMENT ASSETS AND LIABILITIES		
CASH & DEPOSIT ACCOUNTS		
OUTSTANDING DEBT		
RRSPs		
NON - RRSP INVESTMENTS		
OTHER:		
OTHER:		
Total Investment Assets and Liabilities:		
LONG-TERM ASSETS AND LIABILITIES		
PRINCIPAL RESIDENCE		
VEHICLE(S)		
PENSION - DEFINED CONTRIBUTION		
OTHER:		
OTHER:		

Once you have listed your assets and liabilities, calculate the difference.

Assets – Liabilities = Net Financial Worth

When your results are a negative figure, then you have a debt worth the amount in the negative.

While it is never a good feeling to have a debt, it is important to own up to it. This is not the end of the road; we all make mistakes. But the greater evil is to continue repeating the same mistakes. If you are with your children during this process, let them understand that we can always learn from our mistakes, rise above our failures, and soar beyond what we could even imagine.

The other part of knowing ourselves lies in knowing how we spend our money and the resources that are at our disposal. In the next chapter, we will take time to look at our expenditures.

Chapter 3
Knowing Your Expenditures

In addition to knowing just where you are at, you may need to know how you are spending. The key to making a very solid financial plan is to first understand what is taking your money, as well as what you are saving. The business term for this is "tracking your financial flow". This statement is able to give you a clear picture of your spending and saving habits and also inspire confidence in knowing how you can eventually manage your cash flow for the better of your future. You can easily figure out areas that you think you could change and gain financial milestones.

Personally, I have been keeping a journal of my family's expenditures. This helps me know our spending habits, and, whenever we want to achieve a certain desired financial goal, we usually revisit our expenditures and try to see just how comfortably we can carry on and yet achieve the desired financial milestone.

For those who want to get out of debt, I would recommend that if you have not started recording your expenditures, it is high time that you start! When you come back from shopping, sit down and write everything you bought and anything you paid for.

Here is a sample of my expenditure journal; I hope it gives you insight so that you are able to customize and come up with your own.

	Amount		Amount
Your salary		**FIXED EXPENSES**	
Your spouse's salary		➤ Rent/mortgage fee	
Any other source of income		➤ Taxes	
➤ Rental		➤ Insurance	
➤ Investment income		➤ Electricity	
➤ Government benefits		➤ Internet	
		➤ Phone	
		➤ Cable	
		➤ Childcare allowances	
		➤ RRSP	
		➤ RESP	
		➤ Credit card payments	
		➤ Loan repayment	
		➤ Savings	

➢ Car repairs	
Any other fixed expenses	
TOTAL FIXED EXPENSES	
RECURRENT EXPENSES	
➢ Food	
➢ Fuel/gas	
➢ Personal care and hygiene	
➢ Transportation	
➢ Snacks	
➢ Entertainment	
Any other expense	
TOTAL RECURRENT EXPENDITURE	
ANNUAL EXPENDITURE	
➢ Home repairs/maintenance	

	➤ Clothing		
	➤ Medical and dental		
	➤ Professional fees		
	➤ Education/personal improvement		
	➤ Major electronic purchases		
	Any other expense		
	TOTAL ANNUAL EXPENDITURE		
GRAND INCOME TOTAL	GRAND EXPENDITURE TOTAL		
CASH FLOW SURPLUS OR DEFICIT			

For some, this could be quite overwhelming, but this need not be so. And now that you want to get started on your journey to financial freedom, waiting for a whole year to track your expenses may seem like a long time. Thank heaven some of the information you need is readily available. Take, for instance, your expenditure on rent. There are those payments which you can easily remember or find out. Start filling in the above table with the information that is readily available. Once you are done with what is readily available, you can now go for what is not readily available. You see, you simply start from the known and work your way to the unknown. That way, you will gain confidence to finish filling in all the details.

Note

You could choose to find averages for figures that you are not sure about. You could also choose to have another copy of this table so that you keep filling in actual expenditures as your incur them for more accuracy and for future reference.

And now, when you are done filling them in, you can calculate the totals and then find out whether you have a cash flow surplus or a deficit.

To this end, you have a rough idea of where you are. It is important to know where you want to be. Kindly read on to the next chapter to find out where you could be headed in your journey to financial freedom.

Chapter 4
Envisioning Your Financial Future; What is Your Dream?

Each of us is unique, and therefore, it is quite natural to have unique visions or dreams for our futures. One celebrity once said, "Your dreams are valid." And you know that where there is no vision, people perish. You need to have a vision, a dream. Here is a simple exercise to help you with envisioning your future.

Close your eyes. Then imagine that everything went just as you wanted it to go; you have the money you wanted, as well as all the other resources that you wanted; you have the right people and the right amount of time, and everything else went right. Try painting a picture of what your future (10, 20, or 50 years from now) looks like when everything goes right! Where would you want to retire? At what age would you want to retire? What kind of house do you have? What kind of life are you living? What kind of family are you raising? What kind of education have you gone through? And there are many other questions that can help you keep this picture very real in your mind.

This picture makes for a dream for you. Well, I am sure that when you opened your eyes, you were rudely shocked by the reality of your situation. This, for some, could be plain fantasy, but this is your dream and it is valid. The difference lies in your planning to attain your dream. I would encourage you to make the dream crystal-clear and write it down. This starts your journey on the path of what your financial goals are.

While you may not visualize yourself in a $10 million house in Hawaii, you can choose to be more realistic and wish to simply maintain your good living standards into your retirement, ensuring that you keep at bay any financial disasters and have the money to do things you love, like visiting with family and friends. The important thing is to have a dream.

You could have your partner do the same and then compare with each other the results of this exercise. Then, map your dreams together. You may find out that you have similar dreams or different dreams. The bottom line is that both of you have a dream. Discuss both dreams and try to merge them into a family dream, making sure to incorporate each other's ideas. Discuss the values, goals, and lifestyles that you want in your home.

Once you have listed all your goals, you may want to prioritize your goals. So here is a sheet in which we have several financial goals that may interest both you and your partner. Look through the sheet independently, and then compare the results later on.

Financial goals	Rating from least important (1) to most important (5)				
Paying debt (if you have several debts you could prioritize)	1	2	3	4	5
Having control over your expenditures	1	2	3	4	5
Having savings for your children's education	1	2	3	4	5
Having savings for your retirement	1	2	3	4	5
Investing	1	2	3	4	5
Having the same standard of living when retired	1	2	3	4	5
Early retirement	1	2	3	4	5
Cushioning family in the event of your death	1	2	3	4	5
Having an inheritance for the heirs	1	2	3	4	5
Having a legacy upon death	1	2	3	4	5
Buying a house or building one	1	2	3	4	5
Furthering your education	1	2	3	4	5
Buying a car	1	2	3	4	5

Buying other properties	1	2	3	4	5
Philanthropic work/donations	1	2	3	4	5
	1	2	3	4	5
	1	2	3	4	5
	1	2	3	4	5
	1	2	3	4	5
	1	2	3	4	5
	1	2	3	4	5
	1	2	3	4	5
	1	2	3	4	5
	1	2	3	4	5
	1	2	3	4	5
	1	2	3	4	5
	1	2	3	4	5
	1	2	3	4	5
	1	2	3	4	5
	1	2	3	4	5
	1	2	3	4	5
	1	2	3	4	5

Keep listing as many areas of your financial concerns as possible and then talk them over with your spouse. Find out which ones are important to both of you, and reorganize your list in order of priority.

So far, we know where we are and where we want to go! So what's next? Read the next chapter to find out how to proceed from here.

Chapter 5
Merging Your Dreams/Financial Goals with Your Expenditures

Taking a closer look at how you tracked your expenditures versus your income, what was your result? Did you have a positive figure or a negative figure? Well, if you had a negative balance, sorry!!!! That means you are living beyond your means. You will need to revisit your expenditures, as well as your income, to know where the problem could lie. But if you had a positive balance, I say congratulations! Remember, there is always room for improvement. You can always dream bigger every time you think you have reached your dreams. For those who have a negative balance, this is not about laying blame, punishing yourself, or even pointing fingers; it is about knowing the great potential hidden in you, a potential that needs to be analyzed, discovered, and then explored to help you achieve your goals.

When I first took up this challenge, I was simply wondering how I could surmount my $75,000 debt. Then, one afternoon, I was watching cartoons with my children. One cartoon was about a small insect. When he came to the world, he was alone. Then he realized that he had a pair of wings, as well as a paintbrush and a canvas on which to paint! What excited him most were his wings. So he took flight, but he had not gone ten inches before he landed with a thud. The other, older insects were nearby. At first, they were taken aback by this little insect who was up in the air, but, when he came down with a thud, they all laughed at him. Taunting him, they said, "Did you really think you could fly? You are clumsy and nothing more than an insect." He felt bad and moved around with a heavy heart and a bowed head. Somehow, he came to a very beautiful shrub and thought to himself, How wonderful would it be to paint such a shrub? With great enthusiasm, he got down to painting. And, just when he was making great progress, the other insects came along, saying, "You think you can paint? You are clumsy; just look at how you have spoiled your canvas!"

This went on for a while until he sought to be alone, to be away from the negative energy that came from the other insects. He climbed great mountains with much effort, but finally he got to the top. There, he met with an old wise man, the one who had created him. The old wise man explained to the insect that he had given him all he needed to be happy: the wings to fly, and the canvas and the brush to paint beautifully. Feeling encouraged, the little insect realized he really could fly! He soared higher than the eagles and back down to where the other insects were. "We were created to fly and paint beautifully!" he told them. And now that they could see this in him, they all took off for farther destinations and greater heights.

This was enough motivation for me. I was determined to overcome negative energy and explore all that was within my reach to soar to the heights of financial freedom. It can be done. I am sure, if you challenge yourself enough, you will soar higher and higher until you reach your dreams and even supersede them! It is exciting to take up the challenge! Let's do it!

So, we need to align our dreams with the reality of our lives and chart the way forward to our dreams!

As you go through your goals, list the most important of the goals for you and your family. You and your partner should each list your top three goals. If they are the same, then you are good to go, and if they are not the same, review your list and try to reach a compromise. Once you have listed all your goals in order of priority, you will need to compare them to your list of expenditures.

Creatively Reduce Expenditures

Most of us definitely spend money we should not be spending. Well, you need not rush to cut out everything at once; take an item at a time. This way, you will have room to adjust and have breathing space.

Here are a number of things that I started with on cutting expenses:

- Reduced my cable bill expenditure
- Cancelled most of my no-so-healthy magazine subscriptions
- Reduced my budget for going out
- Considered cutting my landline

Say, for instance, you want to buy a cottage in 10 years. You will need to decide whether you want to eat out for those 10 years or save up a part of the money that is used to eat out for the cottage. You owe yourself both current and future happiness. You need to be sincere with yourself as you go through your expenditures. There are those items that you could easily forego without much effort and still achieve a financial milestone. For instance, you could consider cutting out the annual family vacation and replacing it with long weekend camping out with family. The family would still enjoy time out at a nice location, and you would still considerably cut down on your expenses. A friend of mine tried this out, and he was surprised that he was able to save around $4000!

Looking at your expenditures, you may see that you own three cars used by three individuals. The three cars mean more gas, car repairs, insurance, and any other costs that come with having a car. You could consider using two cars, one car, or even choosing to use public transportation. At the end of the day, you have saved on some of the costs that come with the cars and channeled the savings toward clearing your debt.

Build Your Savings

As you start to cut down on your expenditures, you need to have a savings plan ready. Otherwise, you may find yourself spending on things that may not be all that necessary. Now, to this end, it is important to be sincere with yourself and save according to what you are able to save. If you can save only $10 per month, then save that, but if you can save $1000, then do it. Be sure to save something.

I have found out that having a savings account that is different from my usual account can be helpful. Have your savings account linked to your normal account to automatically transfer the amount you chose to save directly to your savings account. You can choose to treat this like any other bill you pay monthly.

So, analyze your spending habits versus your goals, and see what you need to do to achieve your goals and still enjoy your life.

In your prioritization of goals, it is important that, if you have any debts, you prioritize clearing of the debt, along with any other critical goals that you might have. And, as noted in the above paragraphs, do not forget your emergency fund, as well as building your savings. In the next chapter, we will take a look at how to tackle your debt so that you are successfully debt-free.

Chapter 6
Tackling Debt

Do you know that you have all that it takes to tackle your debt? This far, we have been able to analyze your financial standing, as well as your future goals. By now, you know just how much you owe in debts, as well as every detail of your financial life and where you want to go financially. So, where do you start with tackling your debt?

You major milestone in the journey to financial freedom is to start – remember, a journey of a thousand miles starts with one step. At this point, you have already taken several steps in the right direction. One of the milestones towards financial freedom is maintaining a positive attitude, knowing and believing that you can be debt-free. Attitudes influence so much of how we succeed in life. As you think, so you are. Choose to think positively, especially with regard to attaining freedom from debt. There will be circumstances that may cloud your dream of financial freedom, and doubt may engulf you, but you must choose to remain positive and focused. At the start, the amount of debt may be overwhelming, and you may not know whether to clear debt, build your savings, or save for retirement. Well, there may not be any right answer; the important thing is to start moving and take some action!

There are many approaches that one can use to tackle their debt. There are many financial help books that have been written, offering various options for overcoming debt. And, because we are all unique, different methods may work for different people. In this book, we will put forth two options, from which you can choose the one that suits you better. We would also encourage you to read any supplemental materials that seek to shed light on tackling debt. You may not buy into everything they tell you, but you will be sure to find a few gems that will add to your wisdom, as far as debt is concerned.

Top-down Method

The top-down method has been around for a long time. Most financial advisors and finance experts advocate for this method. The reason for this is that it is financially logical. With this method, you take the following steps:

- Arrange your debts from the one with the highest interest rate to the one with the lowest interest rate.
- Decide on the amount of money that you will set aside each month to pay towards the loans.
- Make minimum payments to each of the loans monthly, with the exception of the one with the highest interest rate.
- Every penny that comes in should be thrown at the loan with the highest interest rate.
- Once the loan with the highest interest rate has been cleared, you continue with the same minimum loan payments to the rest of the loans, and throw in every penny at the next available loan with a high interest rate.

So, what does the top-down method for tackling debt involve? Consider the following list of debts:

- $25,000 college loan, 5% interest rate
- $10,000 credit card balance, 12% interest rate
- $5000 car loan, at 4% interest rate

- $1000 computer loan at 10%

If the above list were to be tackled using the top-down method, we would start by first arranging the debts from the one with the highest interest rate to the one with the lowest interest rate.

- $10,000 credit card balance, 12% interest rate
- $1000 computer loan at 10%
- $25,000 college loan, 5% interest rate
- $5000 car loan, at 4% interest rate

As you can see from the above list, this method makes the most financial sense. When one pays off debts with large interest rates, they are able to save so much in terms of the interests that would accrue every month and keep paying the minimal fee possible on the other loans. A better way to look at it is to consider the opportunity cost and the total interest rate that is paid at the end of the loan. If one chose to pay off the smallest debt (in the above list the smallest debt is $1000), then they would pay ($1000 * 10%) $100, while the loan with the highest interest rate would call for ($10,000 * 12%) $1,200. If either of the two loans were to be left to accrue, then one would definitely suffer more in terms of the total interest rate or in the event of defaulting. There would be higher penalties on the one with the highest interest rate, compared to the one with the lowest interest rate.

This method works best for people who have great discipline, those who can stick to the payment schedule until they are finally done with their payments. Apart from the benefits that come with clearing the highest interest rate, anyone choosing to use this method should be aware of the fact that it will take a longer period of time before you can clear your first debt. It therefore calls for perseverance until you are done paying off the loan.

Many of the people we have interacted with say that the debt with the highest interest rate also has the highest balance. It therefore takes a very long time before they see an improvement in their quest to be debt-free. Some attempts have been aborted along the way, while others simply gave up. But if you are the disciplined type, then go ahead! You can be sure that you will spend less to clear all your loans. To help anyone who undertakes tackling debt through this option, it would be wise to calculate just how much you would be saving by using this method so that it serves as a motivator to keep you going until you are done paying your loan.

Bottom-up Method

This method is the one used in the "snowball" theory coined by Dave Ramsey in his book, *Total Money Makeover*. This theory seeks to tackle debt in an interesting way; it focuses on the psychology of clearing debts. With this theory, anyone in debt can choose to ignore the interest rates that are attached to each loan. Instead, individuals focus on the balance of each loan. You then arrange the loans from the lowest balance to the highest balance. In our case, the following would be the order of clearing the loans:

- $1000 computer loan at 10%
- $5000 car loan, at 4% interest rate
- $10,000 credit card balance, 12% interest rate
- $25,000 college loan, 5% interest rate

Once the loans have been arranged in this order, you then choose to pay a minimum balance on all of the loans except the one with the smallest balance. Any money that is in excess, has been saved, has been given as a gift, or any other money that you come across gets thrown into the smallest balance loan. Do this until you are done with the smallest loan. Once you have cleared the smallest loan, you move to the next on the list; in our case, that would be the $5000 loan.

This method receives a lot of praise because of the success stories that come with it. This method offers small psychological reinforcements. Every time an individual is able to clear a loan, they get excited and have more energy to proceed with the next loan. It does not matter how small the loan is; once it is cleared, a very large burden is lifted from one's shoulders. The other dimension in which one could look at the psychological effect is the reduction in the number of people to whom one owes money. This is especially the case if you owe/owed your friends or relatives. The burden to retain friendships and relationships often weighs heavily upon an individual, even if the loan was a very small amount of money. Once such a loan is paid, there is less fretting and more fulfilled social interactions that often become an impetus to accomplish more in life.

While this method has received great acclaim, it has also received criticism in almost equal measure. For some, the mathematics in this method does not seem to add up. The truth about this method of paying off your debt is that you ultimately have to pay more in debt when compared to the person who chose to use the top-down method.

As mentioned earlier, it is important to go with the method that you are more comfortable with, the one that works better for you.

Chapter 7
Have a Strategic Plan

It is not enough to dream; it is not enough to know how much debt you have; it is not enough to have started. After all, the end is better than the beginning of anything. You need to have a strategic plan. This is a document that shows how you intend to reach your final destination financially. It is a plan that captures your vision, mission, and objectives for your financial life. It captures the little steps and actions that you intend to take/do in order to achieve your bigger goals. It also captures any anticipated challenges and what may be the counter-effects of those challenges.

You will need to go back to your goals statement to quantify each of your goals into financial figures or into measurable resources that are needed to achieve those particular goals. With each goal having a financial figure attached to it, you will now need to know just how you intend to raise the money to finance your plan. Say, for instance, you have worked through your debt, and you intend to tackle your $25,000 debt within 5 years. You intend to further your education at a cost of $20,000, and you also want to invest at a cost of $10,000. Thus, you need to know how you will get the money for each of the goals you have.

For most of us, our jobs are the key financiers for our tackling debt and also meeting our goals in life. While this is good, some may need to consider either cutting down on expenditures to create more disposable income or looking for an additional source of income.

Granted, not all the money is needed at the same time. When you go through your plan, you will realize the money is spread out over a given period of time. This gives room for planning, sourcing for income, and even investing money.

A friend of mine, who was working through his plan, thought he needed an additional income if he was to reach his goals. Both he and his wife chose to further their educations and improve their skills so that they could move up the career ladder and get better pay. Thus, they chose to read through relevant materials on the Internet and take available online courses that were relevant to their field. Five years later, their determination paid off. The husband had been promoted three times, and his salary had tripled. His wife had gotten two promotions, which translated to a better income for the couple.

Apart from climbing the corporate ladder, freelancing is one option that would fit in with most people's schedules and still raise considerable amounts of money. Almost every adult in the US owns a computer or a computing gadget. Most adults in the youth age bracket often tend to use their electronic gadgets for entertainment. But such resources as tablets, laptops, and smart phones need not just be used for entertainment. They can also be converted into income-generating gadgets. You could consider doing business online, furthering your education online, and offering services online using the very resources you have at your disposal.

Here are some of the key areas that you will need to focus on when drafting your strategic plan for your financial goals.

Parts of a Strategic Plan for Your Financial Goals

Mission Statement

This is the statement that expresses your purpose in life; you could choose to limit it to your financial life. Every person is unique and has unique experiences that will give them a unique mission statement. While this may seem bothersome, a purpose-driven life is more likely to achieve better results than a life that meanders about without a purpose. Everyone can seek to find out just why they are still alive and write down their purpose. It may not be perfect, but it will drive you to your destination. Your mission statement will definitely shape the rest of your strategies and plans.

Vision Statement

This statement summarizes your dream that was envisioned earlier on in this book. This statement seeks to answer the question, "Where do you intend to be 5, 10, or 50 years down the road?" Make it simple but quite precise. Here is a sample of a vision statement: to be debt-free within five years; to have $50,000 worth of investments in stocks (hotel and tourism sector, agriculture, and housing), to retire 5 years earlier, and to start a project of eradicating hunger in hunger-prone areas 30 years in the future.

Values and Principles

This part of the strategic plan is critical, as it is the backbone of the whole plan. These are your core beliefs that are passionate, enduring, and distinctive. These principles will always play a guiding role in the moments where you are at cross-roads. During times when you want to quit, the enduring principles will remind you of your core values and why you set out on this venture. We encourage you to take some time and list a number of your core values that will support you through this journey to financial freedom. Here are examples of values and principles:

- Have integrity; spend only what you have

- Be yourself; do not follow the bandwagon
- Work hard; work today for your life tomorrow

SWOT Analysis

This is quite simple, but very important. The acronym SWOT stands for Strengths, Weaknesses, Opportunities, and Threats.

For instance, an employed individual with good pay at the end of the month could count their being employed as a **strength**. Better still, one who has more than one source of income could count this as their strength. Strengths are those key elements that will positively impact your strategy.

Opportunities are those avenues through which you can get more income to support your strategies. Opportunities could include making use of a computer for business rather than leisure, making use of your house for a baking business, taking advantage of your vegetable garden to engage in agri-business, and enrolling in a free online course that will positively impact your career growth. Opportunities lie in our networks and in our surroundings. You may have a friend who is a financial expert; this friend could be well placed to give you precise insight on how to go about clearing your debt without incurring any costs. I remember I had a friend who lend me $9000 to clear my car debt upfront and therefore eliminated any other interests that accrued to $1400 over a five-year period. We therefore were left with a local arrangement to pay off the debt at our own pace. So look through your networks and search your environment, and I am sure you will find much leverage for clearing your debt.

Weaknesses are those areas in your life that will undermine the progress of your strategic plan. An example of a weakness is impulse buying. Another weakness is being undisciplined when it comes to time management. This is critical for a full-time freelancer. Freelancers' incomes are directly proportional to the time invested in working. For a freelancer to amass enough income to clear their debts, they need to be disciplined with their time. It would therefore be important to work around your weaknesses and turn them into strengths.

Threats are outside factors that could undermine your strategy. Take, for instance, an increase in the cost of living or taxes. The two would definitely cut down on your disposable income, which then would directly influence the amount of money available to save or clear debts with. In most cases, there is nothing much that you can do to change the threats; maybe you could turn them into opportunities.

Smart Long-term Objectives

Long-term strategic objectives are the key things that must be implemented if you are going to achieve your dream. These long-term objectives span a minimum of three years and could even be lifelong. The acronym "smart" stands for

S – Simple

M – Measurable

A – Attainable

R – Realistic

T – Time-bound

Be sure that all the aspects of "smart" factor in each of your long-term objectives.

Smart Short-Term Actions/Objectives/Initiatives

These are the specific tasks that must be accomplished on a day-to-day basis, which will build up into the long-term objectives that will see your vision come to pass. Make sure that they are "smart."

Score Card

A score card is used to record how well you are performing on your road to financial freedom. It uses key performance indicators to chart how you are performing. Normally, the performance is tracked against weekly, monthly, and yearly targets. It is important to track your performance. Just like so much was revealed when you took a closer look at your expenditures, there is so much that the score card reveals. You are able to see those areas in which you are not performing very well. From such indicators, you may now analyze and see what it is that could have caused such a performance.

Once you gain a better understanding of what could have led to such a performance, you are better placed to make changes that will help you get to your final goal.

There are many resources in terms of easy financial statements that you can make use of to be better placed in being on course towards your financial destination.

Chapter 8
Ways to Watch Out for Wasting Money

Wasting Food

The American society is characterized by wasteful expenditures in many ways. As far as food waste is concerned, so many of us can honestly confess to being part of the grand food wasting scheme. There is hardly any meal that passes without food being wasted, both at home and at food joints. The National Resources Defense Council estimates the amount of food wastage at $165 billion in the US, averaging at $529 per household annually. Reducing such amounts could help you clear your debts in the long run.

Bad Habits

There are so many of us with bad habits, such as eating junk food, drinking excessive amounts of soda, smoking cigars, and imbibing alcohol, among others. Statistics indicate that Americans spent a whopping $2.8 billion on candy last Halloween alone. Fast food claimed a whole $117 billion. Expenditure on alcohol has been found to be $1 for every $100 earned. Smokers of tobacco, especially in New York State, are said to have spent almost a quarter of their income on cigars, due to the high tax levied on tobacco. When considered nationally, 14% of Americans' income has been found to be spent on cigars. The problem with bad habits is that, in the long run, your health is ruined, and you have spent a whole lot more on trying to treat the ailments that result from these bad habits.

Designer Clothing for Babies

One obvious fact about babies is that they grow very fast. Designer clothes are often expensive and, given that the baby will very soon outgrow them, you end up having spent so much money on something that didn't last.

Gambling

On average, an American loses $400 annually to gambling. In 2010 alone, casinos netted $125 billion in gross revenue.

Unclaimed property

There are so many of us in the US who carelessly leave valuable items unclaimed. Examples include stocks, checks, insurance payments, checking accounts, and certificates of deposit, among others.

Unclaimed Tax Refunds

Tax refunds are great sources of income for any individual. Millions of Americans have been found to leave staggering amounts of tax refunds untouched, mostly due to filing taxes on their own. Be sure to make a follow-up on your tax refunds.

Interest on Credit Cards

Statistics show that, on average, a US household owes $15,270, while the whole nation owes $856.9 billion in credit card debt. These statistics are as of January 2014 from the Household Credit Card Debt Statistics. These statistics further indicate that 39% of those holding credit cards need help with a child's college expenses, unemployment income, and out-of-pocket medical allowances.

Most Americans who find themselves with balances need to find out whether they are living beyond their means or if they are just consumers who need assistance.

Wasted Energy

Can you believe a whopping $443 billion is wasted in the form of energy by US households? The suggestions and recommendations on the to-do lists of Americans could actually help Americans save up to a third of their energy costs. We would do well to start training our children on how to save energy. Explore the many ways in which energy is wasted, and work on eliminating such avenues.

Daily Coffee Intake

American workers by Accounting Principles published a recent survey, which claims that, on average, Americans who drink coffee every day end up spending $1092 in a year. Other recent findings from Johns Hopkins Hospital have found that regular intake of coffee is detrimental to an individual's health as well as to their output. It becomes addictive over time so that one cannot function independent of coffee. The drink also begins to undermine the mental capacities so that, with time, there is degeneration of the mental capacities. Medics advise those who may want to quit coffee to take it slowly. Reduce it in small amounts; you could start with reducing half a cup, then a full cup, and, little by little, you will eventually quit. This is because the withdrawal symptoms of coffee could drastically affect the daily operations of an individual who was initially addicted to it. The challenge is worth the effort; you will save money and also save your health.

Speeding and Traffic Tickets

The aftermaths of speeding have often been horrific; many lives have been lost, while millions have endured the grisly accidents that often occur with careless driving. I would prefer that, just for the sake of their lives and property, individuals learn not to speed.

 Research has found out that one in every 6 Americans gets a speeding ticket annually. This translates to 100,000 tickets every day and 41 million tickets in a year. Averaging the cost of a speeding ticket to $150 including court fees, we are spending more than 6 million dollars annually on speeding and other traffic tickets.

Other things one can consider to help avoid the wasting of money include:

- Premium cable packages; for those who may consider reducing expenditures on this item, you could consider a less luxurious package so that you still have the cable package but spend less on it. Many find it hard to just stop having cable, so having a cheaper option would be better.
- Lottery tickets
- Spending on warranties that cost the same as the product for which you are getting the warranty
- Gym memberships that have been unused
- Gift cards that have been unused
- ATM fees that are incurred when an ATM card from a different bank is used to withdraw money

- Opting for speedy shipping even when we are not in a hurry to get the product
- Deal sites

As you can see from the above areas of wastage, there is so much that can be saved towards more noble work and towards investment for the future. These are just a few of the areas that have been found to claim millions of dollars; you are better off looking for other ways through which you could achieve a milestone in your investments, in savings, or in clearing debt. Challenge yourself beyond your comfort zone to ensure maximum usage of whatever resources you have. If possible, look for cheaper ways to achieve the same comfort you are used to, and, if there is no such option, it is better to cut down on your luxuries and have no debt.

Chapter 9
Big Mistakes You Should Not Make

Thinking "Everyone is doing it"-Credit Cards

The bandwagon thinking effect always leaves you at the losing end. One of the ways people get into debt is through the mentality that "everyone is doing it" If, at some point, you find yourself doing something just because others are doing it, then you need to think twice. The American society is full of people with debt. You visit the malls and many are buying the latest gadget, the latest clothing styles, and anything else that appeals to the eye. Many seem to be worried only about increasing their credit limits so that they are able to get all that they need using their credit cards. Credit cards have a way of making it seem so effortless for you to spend money. Not much thought is given to how one will pay off their debt when the bill finally comes in.

Well, the distance you've come in making strides towards being debt-free is commendable. You will need to be wise in your usage of credit cards; after all, credit cards have benefited you in getting such things as an education, a home, and a car, among others. Other benefits of credit cards include getting 1.5%-3.3% discounts, building your credit-worthy status for future major purchases like a home or a car, easy record-keeping for accounting purposes, getting some cash back on your credit cards, and protection from fraudsters. If you are able to manage your credit cards so that you do not carry around balances, then I would not ask you to change your mind. But if you are a victim of balances with your credit cards, you may need to ask yourself questions before you swap your credit card for something less risky. Try using a debit card or cash for the next 14 days, and see how that impacts your expenditures. In situations where you are unable to avoid the usage of credit cards, make sure you pay up whatever you bought using the credit card as soon as possible.

There is a lot that can be said when it comes to how one should use their credit cards; I hope you can find the best way around your credit cards so that they do not pull you back into more debt. Every time you are tempted to have a bandwagon mentality, try thinking, "I will not be at peace until I have cleared my debt."

Do not assume that you can pay off your debt without making a plan for it.

There are so many people who assume that they will just pay off their debt; somehow they think there is no need to sit down and make a plan. This is not only for paying off debt, but also for building your wealth so as to meet your financial goals for your future. It may seem to work, but, with time, you may end up losing on it.

Having a plan is powerful in reaching your desired goals. A plan is like a map that gives you directions at each junction towards your destination. When you do not have a plan, there is a great possibility that you will take the wrong turn at the first junction, then make another wrong one at the next junction, and then you will become completely lost. A personalized and unique plan will, however, show you just how much you need to be laying aside towards your goals. It will also show you the progress that you will be making for each duration of time; you will know if you are not on track and find reasons as to why you are not on track and figure out how to change for the better. With all this information and even more, you will have more energy to press on towards the goals you set for yourself. You are able to celebrate the small milestones that you make towards your big goals.

Remember the saying that the worst handwriting is better than the best memory? That is very true when it comes to tracking your expenditures, savings, and any other elements that touch on your finances. They could be ideas on how to make more money or how to go about clearing your debt, inspirations, or tips. Having written these down, you are better placed to process it in your mind and before you know it, you will find a solution within yourself that is unique to you and that will work for you. Make your journey to financial freedom personal, and that way, you can be sure that it will be great fun.

Negotiating on Rates? What about Debt Settlement Companies?

Negotiating rates is one option many people do not consider, but there is some benefit that you could derive from this option. This is especially for credit card debt, where it is possible to negotiate for lower rates. Just pick up the phone and call your credit card company, asking whether they can negotiate on your debt rates. That sounds simple, doesn't it? But you can save several dollars just by this action.

Medical costs can also be negotiated. You can call up your medical creditor and try to negotiate, especially if you are willing to pay some cash up front. There are those medical suppliers who may consider giving you a lower payment if you start off with cash.

If you reach a moment where you are struggling to pay off such debts as student loans, you should know that there is help if you seek it. There is an option for income-based repayment plans for federal student loans; this will significantly lower your monthly contributions. The other option is to ask for forbearance on your student loans. The same could be applicable for car loans or even credit card loans. Where there is a will, there is a way.

When one is in deep debt, they may want to seek the help of debt settlement companies. Debt settlement companies often negotiate for lower settlements on your behalf. Most debt settlement companies would advise you to first stop paying your monthly pay-offs. This is to make the situation so desperate for your creditors that they readily accept a new and much lower settlement on your account. Sometimes, they are able to help you get as much as 50% off of your settlement. If this becomes the case, you have been saved a large amount of money. But is that all there is to debt settlement? What could be the cons to debt settlement?

While debt settlement promises heaven, it may not be for everyone. I would recommend debt settlement for those who have very low/poor credit ratings. Those going for debt settlement should expect their credit score to be severely damaged for quite some time. When the debt settlement companies tell you to quickly stop paying your monthly installments, what they actually do not tell you is that your creditors will continue to report you to the credit bureaus on late status updates. This may continue for some time until your account goes to collection, is charged off, or is settled. This is the main goal for debt settlement companies. When you now finally settle the debt, your creditors will report it as "settled for lesser than the amount agreed," or in some instances, "settlement as agreed." This will damage your credit report for seven years. The other disadvantage with many debt settlement companies is that they may not be transparent on how much they keep as their fee if the amounts you send them monthly are sent to your creditors.

Last but not least, if you decide to go with a debt settlement company, you may need to countercheck to be sure you are dealing with the right people. You are more at risk working with companies that contact you first instead of your seeking them out. Be sure to read whatever fine print they may have before signing any documents. Check customer reviews and what people are saying about such companies before settling on any one of them. Have as many questions as possible to ask the company during your first meeting.

Having a Wrong Attitude

You know the saying that goes, "A wrong attitude is like a flat tire; it cannot get you anywhere"? You need a complete change of your attitude. In fact, this is the place to start; change your attitude from one of being bogged-down and crumbling under the weight of your debt to a winning attitude. "I can pay off my debts!" should be your attitude.

Chapter 10
Finding Support for Your Journey to Financial Freedom

The wise man said that if you want to fast, then walk alone, but if you want to go far, walk with people. You are destined for financial freedom, and, better yet, you are destined for excellence in your financial life! Finding support for your journey is necessary.

One important thing to remember is that you have a particular dream; you know what you want and where you want to go. This is important so that you are not confused along the way by other people's ideas. They can give moral support, as well as advice, but it is you alone who knows how to sift through all the advice and support and find out which ones help you reach your goals.

There are so many people in debt who may not feel like traveling the rocky path to financial freedom. Such friends may eventually encourage you to give up your quest for financial freedom. You know the proverb that says, "Birds of a feather flock together"? It is important to flock together with those of a similar mindset. Be around people who are talking and thinking financial freedom. Sometimes, you may be the one to start the conversation and you may find that your story is encouraging to someone else.

So, where do you find the necessary support for your journey to financial freedom? There are many avenues through which you can find support. They include but are not limited to the following:

- Family:

    When your family is a partaker of your financial dreams, they usually want to see these dreams come true. Every time you face challenges and every time you have victories, they are there to celebrate and to sympathize with you.

- Friends: Friends greatly influence our lives. When you surround yourself with good friends, you are bound to go places. They help provoke your thinking to invest, to further your education, and to live a better life.

- Personal finance books: Personal finance books are mostly expert advice on how to smartly handle your finances so as to achieve the very best out of your finances. They teach personal finance principles, ways to go about handling debt, investment strategies, and general finance planning. They could be magazines or journal articles; the important thing is that you are exposed to as much information as possible, and then you can add to your wisdom on how you handle your finances.

- Finance websites, forums, and communities: Most of these contain very current information that can impact your financial journey. Forums and communities are especially important, as they contain day-to-day experiences that are shared by other people. These experiences include how they were able to obtain financial freedom, how they were able to invest, and how they are progressing financially. You will definitely leave these sites feeling rejuvenated.

Summary

The journey to financial freedom is the only choice for everyone in financial bondage. There are many who have trodden this path successfully and are now headed for financial greatness. This means that you, too, can walk this path successfully.

The important thing is to follow through on what we have discussed in this book.

- Understand yourself and your enemy; choose life over debt. You are the one in debt, and not any other neighbor or family member. It is best that you take time to look at yourself, your strengths, weaknesses, opportunities, and threats. This forms the beginning of your journey to financial freedom. If you are in debt, admit that you are in debt and make deliberate efforts that will see you out of debt.

- Assess your current financial status so that you know where you are; know your expenditure. Before you get all stressed-out, you need to know your financial standing. This process will certainly reveal to you so many things that you would otherwise not know. You will be able to know just where you money goes, the patterns of your expenditure, what takes the most of your money, and where how to figure your income. From this information, you will be able to know where you need to cut down and where you need to channel your resources. You could also be inspired to see the need for more income. With your mind set to the task, you can be sure to find personal solutions that you may never have come across if you did not take time to go through your finances.

- Identify your dream. Where there is no vision, people perish. A dream gives direction and purpose to your life. It is your desired destination. Having your dream clear and keeping it constantly before you will help you maximize each and every opportunity that comes your way in a bid to meet your goals for your future. Each minute of your time will be spent wisely, knowing that you have things to do if you want to achieve your dream someday. Try envisioning; close your eyes and imagine your dream, as we suggested earlier in the book. In the "Identify Your Dream" section, we included a guide to help you clarify your dream. If you have a family, you could have the rest of your family participate in envisioning their own futures. Once this is done, you should take time to merge the dreams of your family members into one family dream.

- Merge your dreams and your finances. With your dreams merged, take time to reconcile your financial status with your dreams. From where you are financially, how do you intend to move forward to reach your desired dream destination? What are the actions that you need to take in your financial status to enable you reach your dream? You will realize that you may need to wisely cut down on expenditures, build your savings, and tackle your debt.

- Tackle your debt. Debt is the first thing everyone should consider when it comes to finances. It is important to know the extent of your debt. There are many approaches to handling debt; finding the one that works for you is important. There are the top-down and bottom-up approaches. The top-down approach is when you list your debts in order from the one with the highest interest rate to the one with the lowest. You make minimum payments to all other debts with lower interest rates, and then every penny that remains is thrown toward the debt with the highest interest rate. Do this until you clear that debt; then move to the next one with the highest interest rate. The bottom-up approach is when you order your debts from the one with the lowest balance to one with the highest balance. Make minimum payments on the other debts with higher balances, and throw in every last cent to the debt with the lowest balance. Once the debt with the lowest balance is cleared, do the same with the next-lowest balance. The top-down approach is the cheaper of the two. The bottom-up approach is expensive, but gives more satisfaction and determination to continue on with the journey.

- Have a financial strategic plan. Your financial strategic plan is your map to your destination, your dream! This plan is geared towards strategically exploiting every resource and opportunity, while minimizing any threats and weaknesses, for the purposes of achieving your dream. To start with, you will need a vision, a mission, smart objectives, smaller smart objectives, actions, implementation strategies, and monitoring and evaluation strategies. Be sure to follow through with your plan, making adjustments where necessary so that you can consciously reach your destination.

- Cut down on waste. Wasting has long been such a critical part of our society. For many, it may not be such a big deal to throw away a piece of their meal. Putting aside the moral questions that this poses, the true essence of waste (if it is repeatedly done) is that you are throwing away your wealth. Little by little, you will find that you have thrown away a whole lifetime worth of money. Take heed when it comes to wasting.

- Avoid mistakes. Someone said that wisdom is learning from other people's mistakes. When it comes to finances, many have made grave mistakes that have landed them in the deepest of financial pits. You need not tread the same path. You can learn from others' mistakes and have a better journey to financial freedom. Make sure to follow up with what we have included in the eBook, among other things, and you will reach your financial destination.

- Find support; you will definitely need support on your way to your destination. The journey to financial freedom can oftentimes get wearisome. There are times when you might want to give up on your dreams. Finding support ensures that you have the courage to say at the end of the day, "I will try again tomorrow!" With every passing day, you will find renewed strength from your support group to continue on with the journey.

This may not be the whole truth about overcoming debt. With every new day, there is new wisdom that you can keep attaining for your own good. Therefore, keep looking for more and more information until you reach your destination. Face challenges bravely and remember to celebrate your achievements. Stick to your principles in the face of opposition. Monitor and evaluate your progress so that you are always aware of what is happening in your journey to financial freedom. Lastly, think positively.

Appreciation

Thank you for buying this book; you are highly appreciated and valued. We hope that this book will help you reach your greatest dreams just as it has helped others. Feel free to write to us regarding any questions and comments.

www.ingramcontent.com/pod-product-compliance
Lightning Source LLC
Chambersburg PA
CBHW030018190526
45157CB00016B/3128